CHRISTMAS SONGS FOR ALTO SAXOPHONE

Christmas Songs

THAT'S EASY!™

Wise Publications
London/New York/Paris/Sydney/Copenhagen/Madrid

Exclusive Distributors:
Music Sales Limited
8/9 Frith Street, London W1V 5TZ, England.
Music Sales Pty Limited
120 Rothschild Avenue,
Rosebery, NSW 2018, Australia.

This book © Copyright 1994 by
Wise Publications
Order No. AM91971
ISBN 0-7119-4087-8

Music processed by Allegro Reproductions
Designed by Hutton & Partners

Music Sales' complete catalogue describes thousands of titles and is available in full colour sections by subject, direct from
Music Sales Limited. Please state your areas of interest and send a cheque/postal order for £1.50 for postage to:
Music Sales Limited, Newmarket Road, Bury St. Edmunds, Suffolk IP33 3YB.

Your Guarantee of Quality
As publishers, we strive to produce every book to the highest commercial standards.

The music has been freshly engraved and the book has been carefully designed to minimise
awkward page turns and to make playing from it a real pleasure.

Particular care has been given to specifying acid-free, neutral-sized paper made from pulps which have not been
elemental chlorine bleached. This pulp is from farmed sustainable forests and was produced with special regard for the
environment. Throughout, the printing and binding have been planned to ensure a sturdy, attractive publication
which should give years of enjoyment.

If your copy fails to meet our high standards, please inform us and we will gladly replace it.

Printed in the United Kingdom by
Caligraving Limited, Thetford, Norfolk.

CONTENTS

A Root'n Toot'n Santa Claus

Words & Music by Oakley Haldeman & Peter Tinturin

Carol Of The Drum

Words & Music by Katherine K. Davies

Christmas Alphabet

Words & Music by Buddy Kaye & Jules Loman

Deck The Halls

Traditional

Jolly

Ding Dong Merrily On High

Traditional

Frosty The Snowman

Words & Music by Steve Nelson & Jack Rollins

Happy Xmas (War Is Over)

Words & Music by John Lennon & Yoko Ono

Good King Wenceslas

Traditional Christmas Carol

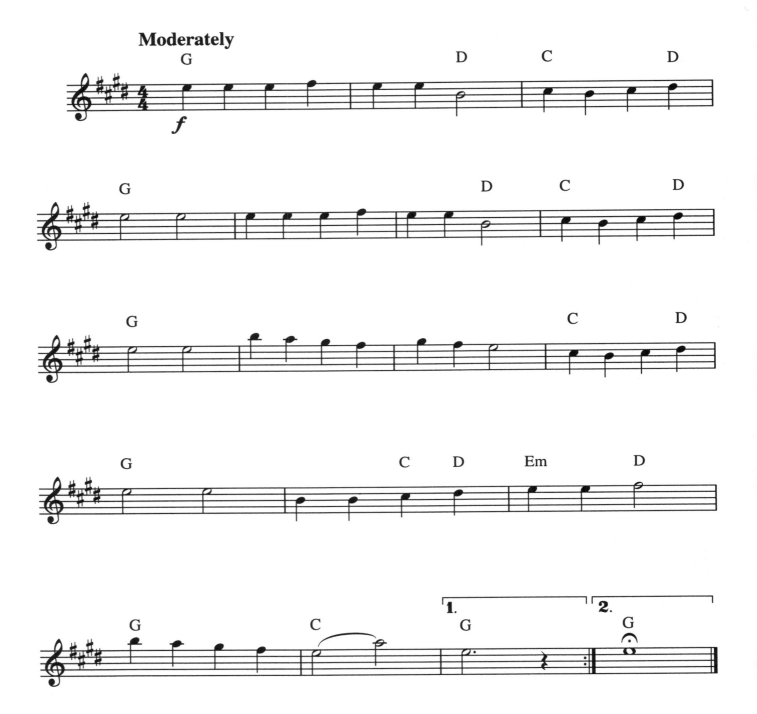

Hark! The Herald Angels Sing

Christmas Carol

Here Comes Santa Claus

Words & Music by Gene Autry & Oakley Haldeman

Jingle Bells

Traditional

Let There Be Peace On Earth

Words & Music by Sy Miller & Jill Jackson

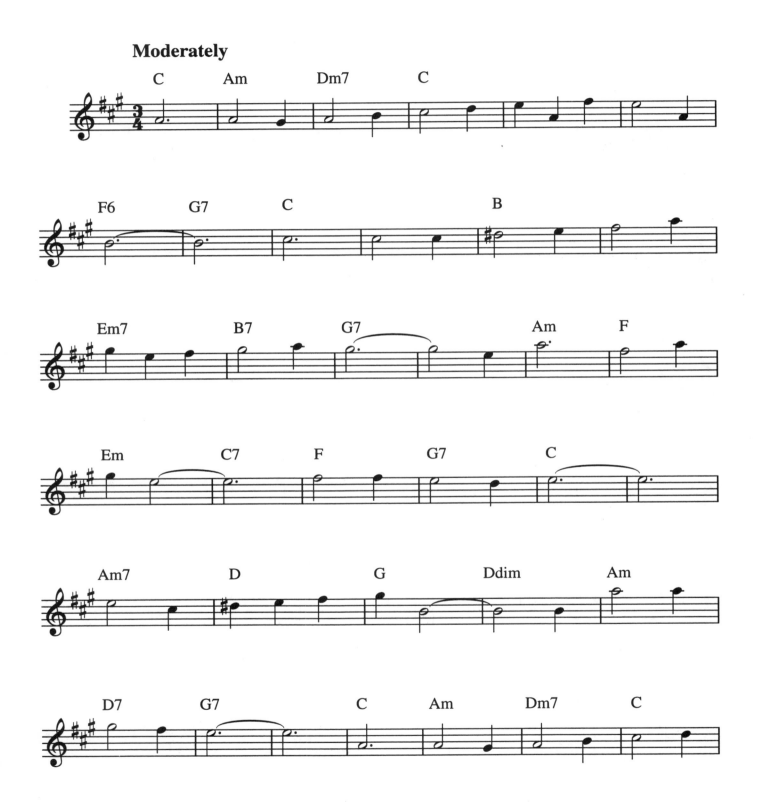

Mary's Boy Child

Words & Music by Jester Hairston

O Christmas Tree (O Tannenbaum)

Christmas Carol

Merry Xmas Everybody

Words & Music by Neville Holder & James Lea

O Come All Ye Faithful

Traditional

O Little Town Of Bethlehem

Anonymous

Moderately

Once In Royal David's City

Traditional Christmas Carol

Moderately

Silent Night

Words & Music by Joseph Mohr & Franz Gruber

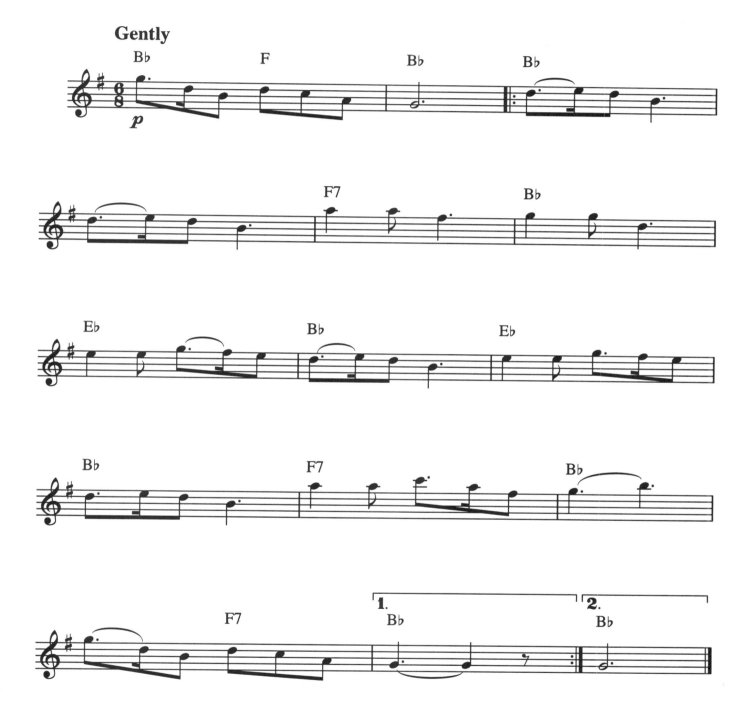

The First Nowell

Traditional

With movement

The Holly And The Ivy

Traditional

With movement

The Twelve Days Of Christmas

Traditional Christmas Song

We Three Kings Of Orient Are

Traditional

Moderately

While Shepherds Watched Their Flocks

Traditional

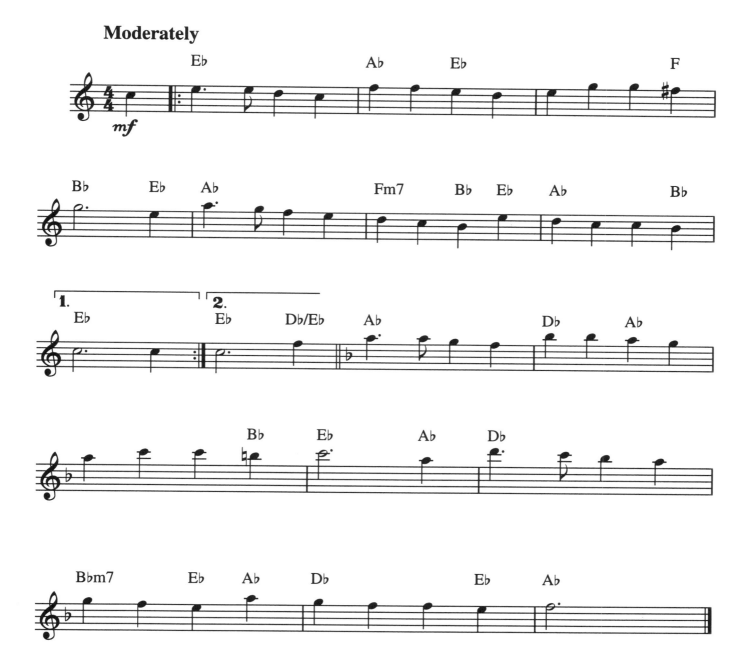

The Beatles

Enya

Phil Collins

Van Morrison

Bob Dylan

Sting

Paul Simon

Tracy Chapman

Eric Clapton

Pink Floyd

New Kids On The Block

Bryan Adams

Tina Turner

Elton John

Bee Gees

Whitney Houston

AC/DC

Bringing you the words

All the latest in rock and pop. Plus the brightest and best in West End show scores. Music books for every instrument under the sun. And exciting new teach-yourself ideas like "Let's Play Keyboard" - in cassette/book packs, or on video. Available from all good music shops.

and music

Music Sales' complete catalogue lists thousands of titles and is available free from your local music shop, or direct from Music Sales Limited. Please send a cheque or postal order for £1.50 (for postage) to:

Music Sales Limited
Newmarket Road,
Bury St Edmunds,
Suffolk IP33 3YB

Buddy

Five Guys Named Moe

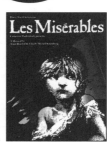
Les Misérables

West Side Story

Phantom Of The Opera

Show Boat

The Rocky Horror Show

Bringing you the world's best music.